The Circles

Kerry Armstrong

Paintings by Deborah Russell

Mandala by Emma Samin

ATRIA BOOKS
New York London Toronto Sydney

BEYOND WORDS
PUBLISHING

ATRIA BOOKS

A Division of Simon & Schuster, Inc.
1230 Avenue of the Americas
New York, NY 10020

BEYOND WORDS

PUBLISHING

20827 N.W. Cornell Road, Suite 500
Hillsboro, Oregon 97124-9808
503-531-8700 / 503-531-8773 fax
www.beyondword.com

Paintings: Deborah Russell
Mandala: Emma Samin
Cover: Kate Mitchell Design
Interior design/composition: text-art

First Atria Books/Beyond Words hardcover edition May 2008

ATRIA BOOKS and colophon are trademarks of Simon & Schuster, Inc.
Beyond Words Publishing is a division of Simon & Schuster, Inc.

For more information about special discounts for bulk purchases, please contact Simon & Schuster Special
Sales at 1-800-456-6798 or business@simonandschuster.com.

Manufactured in China

10 9 8 7 6 5 4 3 2 1

Library of Congress Cataloging-in-Publication Data:

Armstrong, Kerry,
  The circles / Kerry Armstrong. -- 1st Atria Books/Beyond Words hardcover ed.
    p.   cm.
  Originally published: Victoria, Australia : Hardie Grant Books, 2003.
  1. Self-perception. 2. Interpersonal relations. I. Title.

  BF697.5.S43A76 2008
  158.2--dc22

                              2007050936

ISBN-13: 978-1-58270-203-2
ISBN-10:   1-58270-203-9

The corporate mission of Beyond Words Publishing, Inc.: *Inspire to Integrity*

It is only with the heart that one can see rightly.

What is essential is invisible to the eye.

ANTOINE DE SAINT-EXUPERY, *The Little Prince*

Contents

this book
is an
offering

It came out of a moment of great simplicity.

Sitting on my veranda,
looking back over the events
and people in my life,
I realized I had
come to a clearing.

A resting place.

And out of that clarity
came the realization that
I was in a new place.

It felt fantastic.

I had finally let go of despair,
blame, judgment, fear, and shame.

I had found a way through the
endless cycle of wondering
what people were thinking of me,
why they didn't get me,
how I could prove myself,
explain myself, or
show them who I really am.

I knew that I could finally stop . . .

. . .worrying.

And start to live my life in a different way.
But I didn't have to become a different person.

I just had to realize how to not only *be* me,
but how to let myself *be*.

And let everyone else in my life just be.

This is how I found

The Circles.

What are
The Circles?

Plato said that the soul is a Circle.

JOSEPH CAMPBELL, *The Power of Myth*

The Circles are a practical exercise to help
you sort out your feelings.

There are seven circles inside
one main circle.

All seven circles represent you.
Your life.

They are a bird's eye view of
who you are and how you feel.

Each of the seven circles represents
where people are in your life.
Your relationships with them.

You write down the names of people
in your life according to where they fit in.

The Circles are about
living in the moment.

They are not permanent.

Feelings change, people come and go.

The Circles will reflect these changes.

You begin by writing down in the first
circle those who make you feel good
about yourself.

Move out through circles
two, three, four and so on.

Finally, write down the people
you find most challenging in the
seventh circle…

By putting our feelings

and thoughts about

people in front of us,

we can see how we feel

about our relationships

with them.

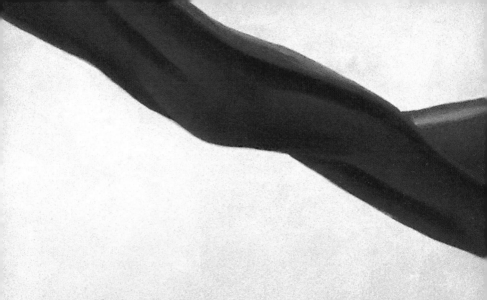

The Circles give us freedom to enjoy those who
make us feel good. Space to handle difficult relationships
and help get rid of feelings that weigh us down.

You may find the resulting clarity liberating.

Why?

We all want to feel good about ourselves.
But sometimes we don't.

Sometimes, how we feel about ourselves
depends on how we let other people affect us.

You can't force someone to like you.
Belonging to a group where you feel afraid
to be yourself can be unsettling,
sometimes even humiliating.

You may end up feeling lonelier with the
wrong people than you did on your own.
You might lose your way, try to change.
Do things that you know aren't right for you.
Or give away the very part of yourself
that makes you …

you.

Sometimes it takes years to learn
how to look after yourself.

That's why it's important to have people
around you who love you well.

Sometimes, even more than
you can love yourself.

Shrug off the restraints that you have
allowed others to place upon you.

CLEARWATER

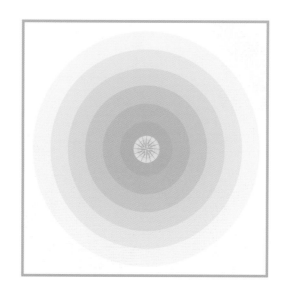

Doing
The Circles

1 Find a piece of paper, and a pen or pencil.
2 On the piece of paper, draw the seven circles.
3 Write down the numbers from 1 to 7, beginning with the number 1 in the center and working outward to number 7.
4 Give yourself enough space for names. You can use either initials, first names, or surnames.
5 Give yourself some time to think about your life, and the people in it—your family, friends, workmates, lovers.
6 You don't have to have a name in every circle. There can be more than one person in a circle.
7 You can change names and places whenever you want to. Nothing is permanent.
Feelings change.

Ask yourself . . .

How does this person make me feel?
Can I be myself with them?

Am I honest with them?
Can I say what I want to?

Do I feel comfortable with them?

How do I feel when this person
walks into a room?

How do I feel when this person leaves?

Do I change myself for them?
Do I want them to change for me?

Do I hide my real feelings or am
I open when I'm with them?

Do they make me feel less or
more than I am?

Do I trust them?

The Circles
are about

recognition,

not judgement.

Be honest with yourself.

Take your time with people you find difficult.

Try not to place someone in a particular circle because you think you should place them there.

Even though you spend a lot of time with a person, whether it be at work, at home, or socially, they don't have to be in the first three circles.

The wonderful thing about The Circles
is that they are yours and yours alone.

No one can suggest or tell you where to put someone.

The seven circles make up one larger circle.

One life.

Yours.

I

The First Circle

one   uno   yi   un   uno   ichi

This is the center. The Self.

The place where you feel

strongest and true.

The place you put people

you trust with your

heart and soul.

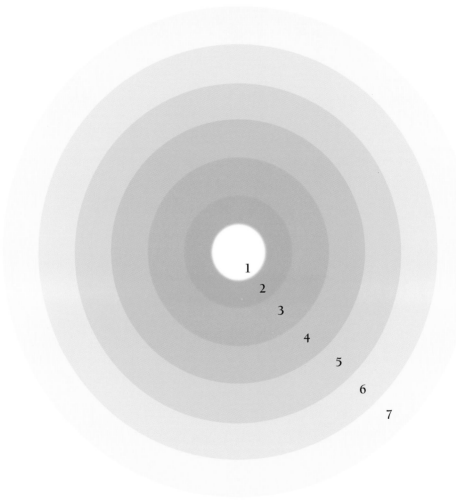

The First Circle is where you get to express
all your hopes, dreams, and thoughts.
Take a moment to stop worrying.
Doubting.
And just be.
Put yourself in the center and
ask yourself:
who knows me here?
Who can I trust with my life,
my thoughts, my dreams?
Who makes me feel free to be myself?

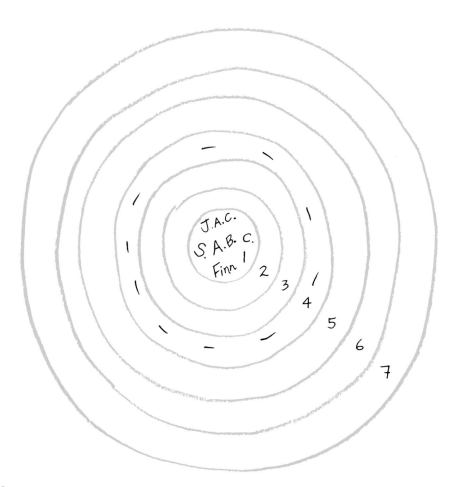

J.A.C.
S. A.B. C.
Finn 1
2
3
4
5
6
7

You may find it easy to put a few
names in the center.
You may realize that is a place that
only you can be in.
You may find that it doesn't feel right to
put the name of a close friend or relative.
Don't worry. Trust your instincts.

The Circles are only momentary.

You can change your mind at any time.
Don't let guilt or fear dictate your choices.
This exercise is to find out how you feel.

Trust yourself.

Some people find it hard to put themselves
in the center when they feel fearful,
angry, or cannot love themselves.

Be patient.

Take your time.

2

The Second Circle

two   dos   er   deux   due   ni

You feel happy and strong

with people in the Second Circle.

These are people with whom

you have shared values.

Wonderful friends.

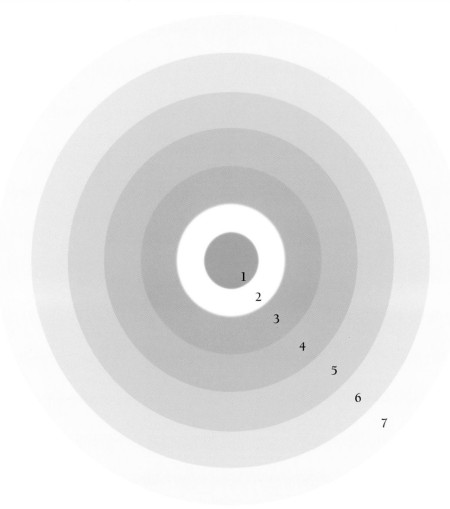

Circle Two represents:

Balance. Stability. Ease.

44

By understanding how others make you feel,
you can get free of these feelings.

Once you can see what you are thinking,
you may untie
some of the knots.

3

The Third Circle

three   tres   san   trois   tre   san

They may be acquaintances,

friends, or family.

Mentors or teachers.

They help you grow.

You respect them.

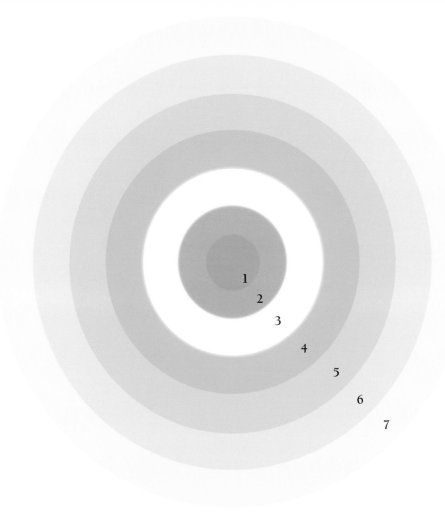

The people in the Third Circle
may be wonderful to spend time with,
even though you may not see them often.
They may be people who have
moved out of your inner circle,
but whom you still
enjoy and feel good about.

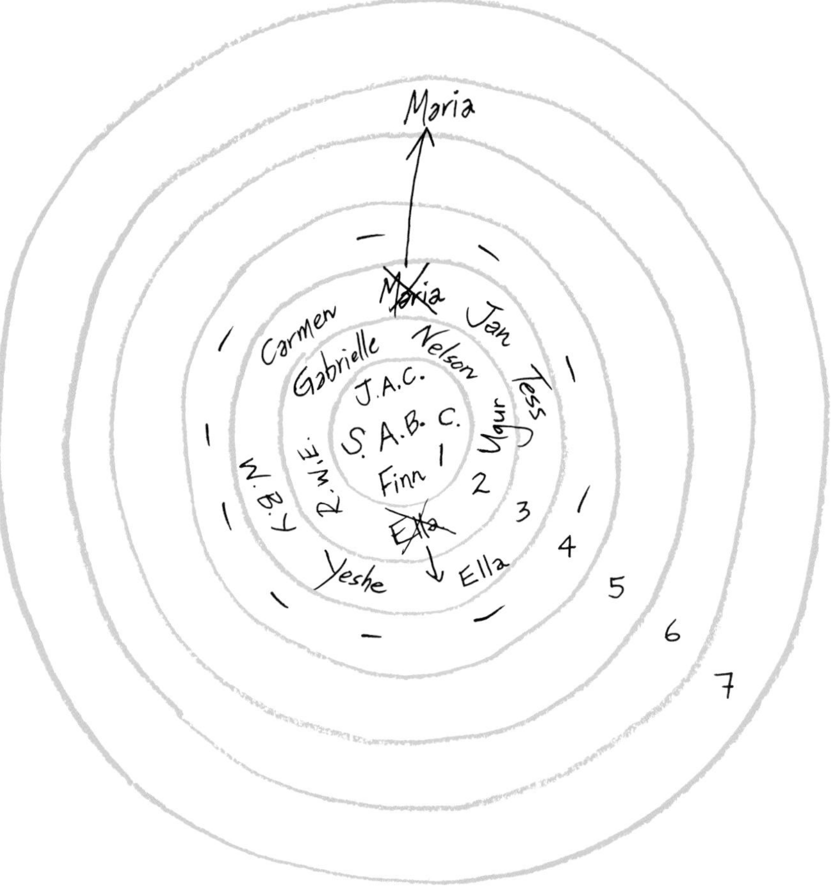

Maria
~~Maria~~
Carmen
Jan
Gabrielle
Nelson
Tess
J.A.C.
S.A.B.C.
Ugur
Finn
1
2
R.W.E.
W.B.Y.
3
~~Ella~~
4
Yeshe
Ella
5
6
7

Kindness is more important than wisdom,
and the recognition of this is the
beginning of wisdom.

THEODORE ISAAC RUBIN

4

The Fourth Circle

four   cuatro   si   quatre   quattro   shi

These are the Moving Lines.

This is the place where you can put

people you have just met.

The Fourth Circle gives you

time to think.

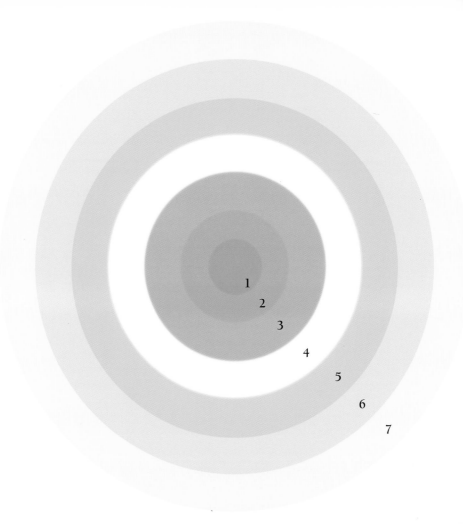

The Fourth Circle can help you

bide your time.

Withhold judgment.

The Fourth Circle is neutral.

The people here are either coming in

or going out.

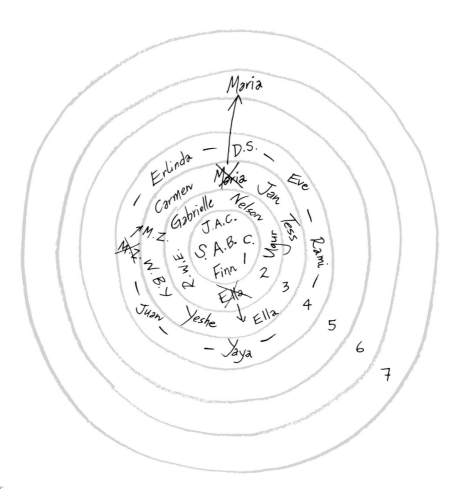

I had found a kind of serenity, a new
maturity . . . I didn't feel better or stronger
than anyone else but it seemed no longer
important whether everyone loved me or not—
more important now was for me to love them.
Feeling that way turns your whole life around;
living becomes the act of giving.

BEVERLY SILLS

5

The Fifth Circle

five   cinco   wu   cinq   cinque   go

The Fifth Circle is the beginning

of your strength and resolve.

This is where you put people who

are holding you back.

The people here are not necessarily

connected with the real you.

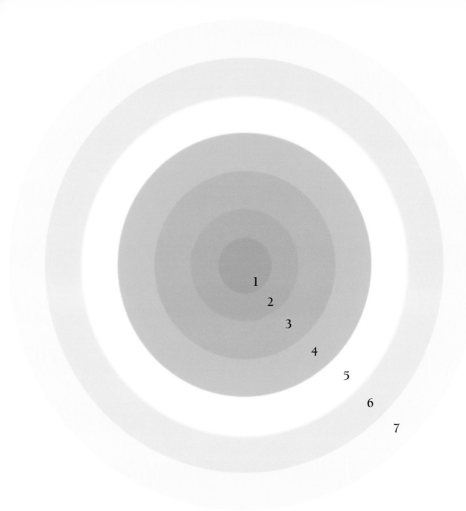

The Fifth Circle gives you the chance
to stop explaining yourself,
and to let go
of feelings of inadequacy.

People in the Fifth Circle may also be moving
closer to your center, after having been
in the Sixth or Seventh Circle.

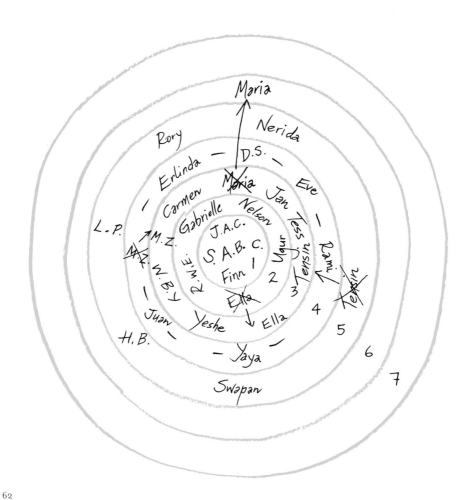

62

My children have asked me, "But what if
they make me feel bad, Mummy?"
And I have said to them, "It is a choice.
No one can make you feel anything
unless you let them."

The Circles may help you stop
blaming others.

6

The Sixth Circle

six   seis   liu   six   sei   roku

The Sixth Circle is where you create

a sense of release.

People here may seem important

to you, your career, or

in your social life, but try as you will,

you cannot feel comfortable with them.

Unable to feel close to them,

they unsettle you when you see them.

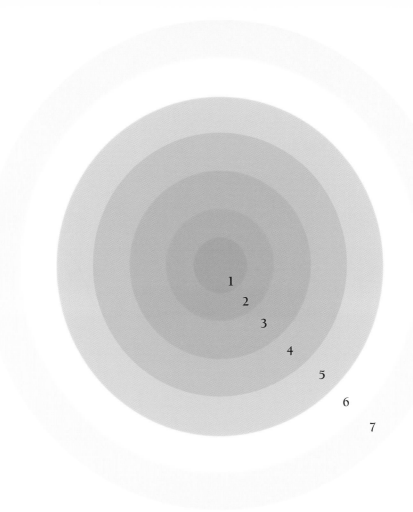

The Sixth Circle is a chance to
redefine how you see yourself.
This is where your frustration over
someone can be softened.
From here, you may begin to open your heart
to people you have "given up" on.

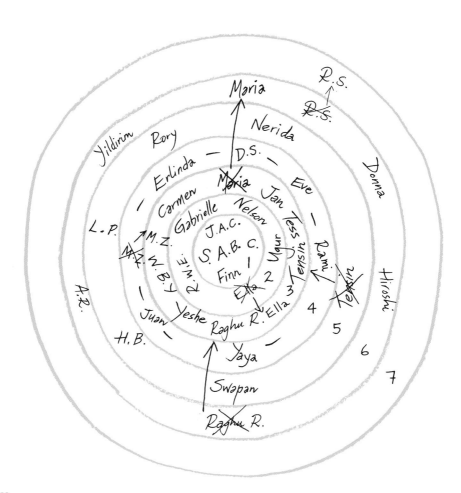

Sometimes we take people who love us for granted and spend more energy trying to please or impress new and "exciting" people.

7

The Seventh Circle

seven   siete   qi   sept   sette   nana

The Seventh Circle is the furthest out.

This is where you place people who

have hurt you, angered you, or let you down.

From here you can start

letting go of painful thoughts and feelings.

The Seventh Circle may help you

find your center again.

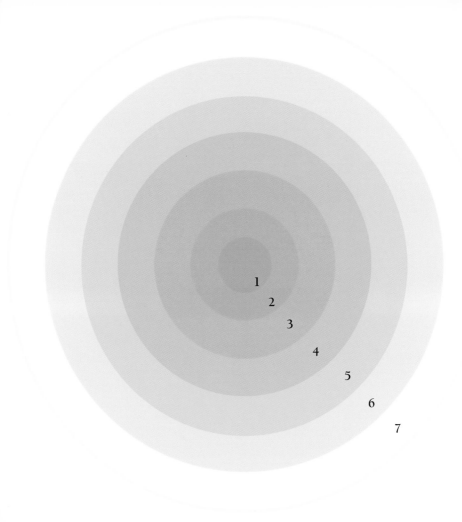

Some people have asked why there isn't
a seventeenth circle, or a seventieth, or a
circle that is so far away that you don't have to
face it or think about it.
But this is where The Circles stop.
The distance that the Seventh Circle
gives you can heal anger and emotional
illnesses that wear you down.

The positive aspect of
the Seventh Circle can help you
find rest and release.

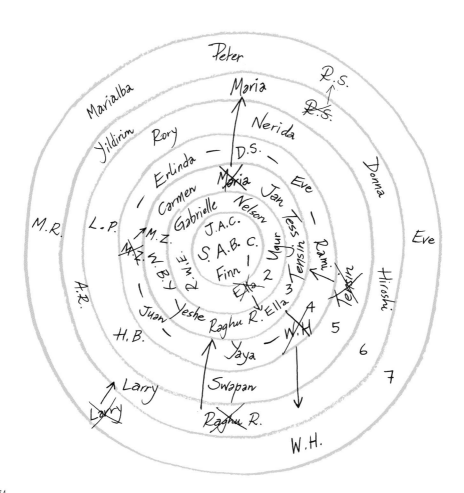

You can transcend all negativity when you
realize that the only power it has over you is
your belief in it. As you experience this truth
about yourself, you are set free.

EILEEN CADDY

The Seven Circles: A Guide

First

This is the center, the place you put the people you trust with your heart and soul. It is the beginning of your tribe. (Some people may not want to put anyone here—that's fine, too.)

Second

You feel happy and strong with people in the second circle. These are people with whom you have shared values. Wonderful friends, even if you don't always understand each other.

Third

People you respect, who may be friends, family, or acquaintances. You feel positive in their company. They may be people you are not as close to, but you still enjoy and feel good about them.

Fourth

These are the Moving Lines. The fourth circle gives you time to rest, to find order. This is where you can put people you've just met. You may feel that they are moving to the inner circles or moving out.

Fifth

This is where you put people who are holding you back.
They may have moved from Circles Three or Four to here,
a safe distance from your center. The people here are not
necessarily connected with the real you.

Sixth

They may be people you believe are important to you, your
career, or in your social life, but try as you will, you cannot
feel comfortable with them. You are unable to feel close to
them. Circle Six gives you the chance to let go of feelings
of inadequacy and to stop explaining yourself.

Seventh

The Seventh Circle is the furthest out. The distance of the
Seventh Circle from the center gives you rest and release.
This is where you place people who hurt you, angered you,
or let you down. From here you can start letting go of
painful thoughts and feelings.

Benefit others. If you can't benefit others,
at least don't harm them.

DALAI LAMA

The Circles
in Your Family

Families can be wonderful. The place where we find unconditional love and endless support. Our own personal cheer squad. Our closest friends.

Families can also be the most challenging parts of our lives. They can be confusing, frustrating, depleting, and sometimes even cruel.

Some of the largest shifts in The Circles have been with people who have felt pressure to keep family members in their inner circles. They think they are being disloyal if they move family members beyond the first three circles.

Sometimes it takes a little while and a lot of courage before the shift begins.

Remember, this is not a permanent exercise, nor is it meant to be judgmental.

Family members have a very strong view of you. They tend to believe that their view is the right one. The trouble is, they usually need to be slightly "above" you to have this viewpoint.

This is where it gets a little difficult. Yes, they know you well, but you may have changed, quite a lot. They may not have noticed the changes or have not changed much themselves, so they keep relating to you in the same way.

Try as you may, they will not let go of their out-dated version of "you." Often because they don't want to, or can't.

Placing these family members further out may give you a chance to find rest, release, and clarity. You may find it easier to be with them.

You may start to
heal old wounds.

The Circles
with Friends

A friend may well be reckoned
the masterpiece of nature.

RALPH WALDO EMERSON

Friendship is a gift.

A wonderful part of life. An unexpected surprise.

A friend is a companion, someone you can talk to, who'll listen and laugh with you.

A true friend won't let you down, but will help you through the rough bits, and carry you through the times when you think you can't go on.

A friend will back you up, won't run you down, or talk behind your back.

A friend will love you and your loved ones, but would never take advantage of you or betray you.

A friend will keep your innermost secrets safe.

Value your beliefs, your dreams.

Uphold and honor your morals.

Understand you.

And let you be yourself.

And then there are the people who say they are
your friends, but:
Undermine you.
Deplete you.
Let you down.
Try to change you.
Take away your faith in yourself.

In times like these,
The Circles may help.

The Circles
at Work

Wherever you work, there will always be good and bad days.

The workplace is where we can be productive, creative, intelligent, useful, in charge. To earn a living, be recognized for all our hard work.

For some of us, going to work can be the opposite. Work becomes the thing we dread, a place where we struggle to be heard, where we work hard for seemingly little reward.

The most frustrating part of your day may be a person you have to work with, and too much time and energy is spent thinking about them.

The Circles may help you with circumstances at work that seem insurmountable.

The Circles are helping me find my way.

Where there was confusion,
I now have clarity;
where there was despair, I now find hope.
And where I was held to ransom by so many
people, including myself,
I now have freedom.

I wish you the same.

Where we had thought to travel outward, we will come to the center of our own existence. And where we had thought to be alone, we will be with all the world.

JOSEPH CAMPBELL, *The Power of Myth*

Thanks & Acknowledgments

Sam

My heartfelt thanks to everyone at Beyond Words, especially Cynthia Black for her enthusiasm and innate understanding, Richard Cohn, Courtney Dunham, Marie Hix, Michele Ashtiani, Sara Blum, and Lindsay Brown. Thanks also to Judith Curr for her support.

I am grateful to so many people for their guidance: Phillip Adams, Katia and Sylvio Ascenzo, Chris Beck, Paul Bell, Andrew Best, Mario Borg, Cara Britton, Kirsty Cockburn, Helen Coleman, Marisa Colosimo-Dinardo and Angelo Dinardo, Robina Courtin, Mark Davis, Lorraine Edwards, Jon Faine, Tara Ferrier, Mac Gudgeon, Helen & Wayne Lacelles, Ian Loughnan, George Negus, James Oldham, Jane Palfreyman, Petra Reece, Jan Sardi, Margie Skeggs, Kerrie Theobald, Rick Thompson, Andrew Tilley, Sue Turnbull, Yasmine, Rachel Walton, Jane Watson, Petra Yared and Peter Mews from Brunswick Street Bookstore for his encouragement.

Jai

Special thanks to:

Sandy Grant and the brilliant team at Hardie Grant. To Katie Mitchell for the cover design, Nina Landis for her photograph, Emma Samin for her Mandalas and Deborah Russell for her sublime paintings.

Nu and Kim Lynch, who helped begin the journey.

My amazing friends Rebecca Gibney and Richard Bell, who gathered me in when I most needed it.

Foong Ling Kong, who wanted me to love the making of this little book—thanks for your brilliant clarity.

My extraordinary agent and dear friend, Barbara Leane.

My God-sent PA and nanny Lily Brocksopp—my respect for you knows no boundaries.

My beloved parents Beverley and Norman Armstrong, and my beautiful sister Kim, whose support is endless.

My children Sam, Jai, Callum and my stepdaughter Shanti, who fill my life with more joy than I could possibly imagine.

And finally to my brother Mark Armstrong, who never wavered from beginning to end, and without whom the book wouldn't exist.

you Dont always find your way by your brain Sometimes you have to find your way with your heart

Callum

Kerry Armstrong is mother to Sam, Jai and Callum, and the stepmother of Shanti.

Kerry is an acclaimed actor, and has worked internationally. She made history in Australia in 2001, winning both the AFI Awards for Best Actress in film and television for the ABC television series *SeaChange* and for her performance in the feature film *Lantana*.

Kerry is spokesperson for Cure for Life and is ambassador for Child Wise Australia. She also supports Kids Under Cover, and is a founding member of Big hArt, the award-winning company renowned for its work with young adults.

In 2003 Kerry was awarded the Centennial Medal for Culture.

The Circles is her first book.

Photograph © Nina Landis